WARRIORS

WARRIORS
Navajo Code Talkers

PHOTOGRAPHS BY KENJI KAWANO

FOREWORD BY CARL GORMAN, CODE TALKER ★ INTRODUCTION BY BENIS M. FRANK, USMC

Northland Publishing

www.northlandbooks.com

Manufactured and Printed in the United States of America

First Impression, 1991

05   06   07   08   09   19   18   17   16

ISBN 13: 978-0-87358-513-2 (pb)
ISBN 10: 0-87358-513-5 (pb)

Library of Congress Cataloging-in-Publication Data
Kawano, Kenji,
Warriors: Navajo code talkers/photographs by Kenji Kawano;
foreword by Carl Gorman: introduction by Benis M. Frank.
—1st ed. 128p.
1. World War, 1939–1945–Cryptography. 2. Navajo language.
3. World War, 1939–1945–Indians–Portraits. 4. Navajo Indians–Portraits.
5. United States–Military services–Indian troops–Portraits. 1. Title.
D810.C88K38   1990   90-53285
940.54'03-dc20

COVER: William Dean Wilson in front of the U.S. Marine Corps monument,
Washington, D.C., 1983.

FRONTISPIECE: Cpt. Henry Bake Jr. (left) and Pfc. George H. Kirk (right), Navajo Indians
serving with a Marine Signal Unit, operated a portable radio set in a clearing they backed in
the dense jungle, close behind the front line, Bougainville, December 1943.

PHOTOGRAPH COURTESY U.S. MARINE CORPS, NO. 69889-A

To my parents, Mr. and Mrs. Yukio Kawano,
and the Navajo code talkers and their families.

CONTENTS

FOREWORD

IT WAS ABOUT FIFTEEN YEARS AGO that I saw a man walking along the road in Window Rock, Arizona. He was carrying a big camera bag over his shoulder. I stopped my car and asked if he'd like a lift to St. Michaels, Arizona, about two miles along the way. I learned that his name was Kenji Kawano, he was from Japan, and was staying in Ganado, Arizona. Ganado is close to thirty miles west of where we were, but he accepted my invitation to go with my wife and I to a Squaw Dance (Enemy Way Ceremony) in Crystal, New Mexico. Getting back to Ganado could wait.

ABOVE: *Carl N. Gorman (left) and Eugene R. Crawford (right), two of the original twenty-nine code talkers; photograph taken at Fort Defiance, Arizona, 1987.*

Every time after that, when I saw him walking along the road, I picked him up. He was always going here and there keeping his eyes open for pictures of the country and the Navajo people who inspired him as subjects. Our friendship grew and now he, his wife Ruth, and daughter Sakura, are like family to my wife and I.

Sometime shortly after we met, Kenji learned that I had been a Navajo code talker in the Marine Corps in World War II. Our Navajo language had been coded and used very successfully in the Pacific in the battles with the Japanese forces. One day, I took him to a Navajo Code Talkers Association meeting. He began taking pictures of us in parades and functions where we appeared. He then became a photographer for the *Navajo Times* and began accompanying us to parades and special functions where

OPPOSITE: *Pfc. Carl N. Gorman mans an observation post on a hill overlooking the city of Garapan as the Marines consolidated their positions on the island of Saipan, June 27, 1944.*
PHOTOGRAPH COURTESY U.S. MARINE CORPS.

we appeared or were honored. We made him "official" photographer for the association and, later, an honorary member.

Sometimes he would travel on the bus to Phoenix or San Diego. He

ABOVE: *Code talkers proudly carrying the flags of the United States, the Navajo Nation, the State of Arizona, the State of New Mexico, and their group during a parade.*

RIGHT: *Navajo Indian Marines on Saipan landed with the first assault waves to hit the beach. (Left to right) Cpl. Oscar B. Iithma, Gallup, New Mexico; Pfc. Jack Nez, Fort Defiance, Arizona; and Pfc. Carl N. Gorman, Chinle, Arizona.*

PHOTOGRAPH COURTESY U.S. MARINE CORPS, NO. 82619.

had a great opportunity there to talk with many of the code talkers. He became well-acquainted with many of us. As a sensitive photographer, he had a good chance on these trips to observe us. The portrait photos in this book reflect years of contact with us as individuals as we are today, and something of who we were forty years ago when our language helped the United States defeat his people.

Kenji must have thought many times about how he happened to be photographing the code talkers. Somewhere along the line, he decided he wanted his people to know about the code talkers. He wanted them to know that the Navajo language code that had baffled their communicators was created by people who looked so much like them that some of our Navajo Marines were even mistaken for Japanese by our own American soldiers. More than this, he wanted the American people to know more about us. He decided to do a book that would honor us. Kenji Kawano's portraits speak for themselves. They also say volumes about the man, as you will see.

As our friendship began with a visit to a Navajo Enemy Way Ceremony, so does this book and tribute symbolize the healing of the wounds of war. To Kenji Kawano, my Japanese-Navajo friend, I say *ahéhee* (thank you).

Carl N. Gorman, Code Talker
Window Rock, Arizona

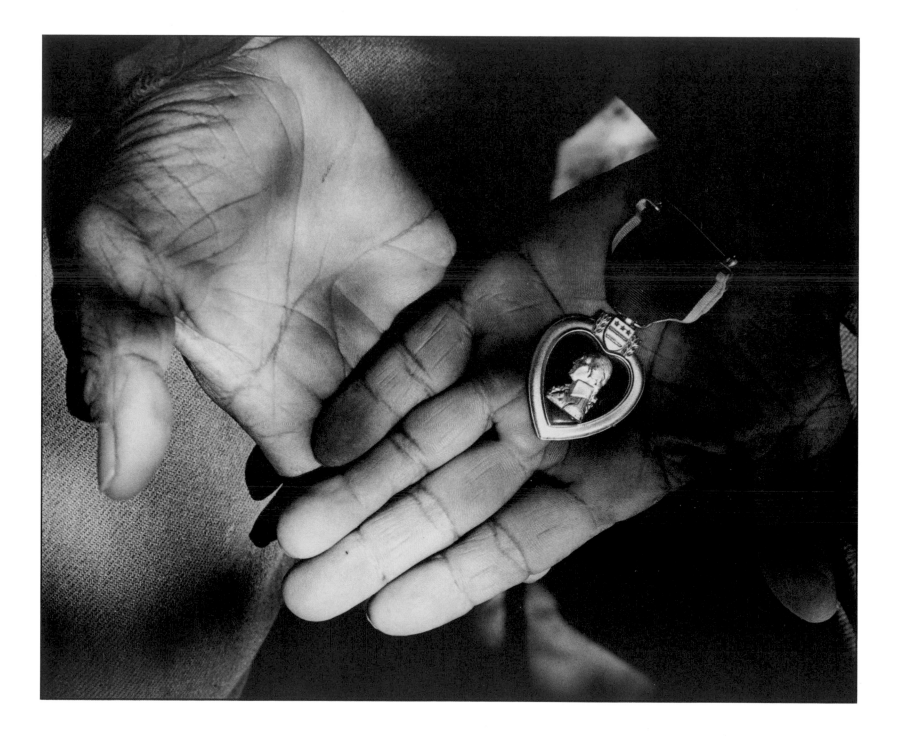

PREFACE

WHEN I WAS LIVING IN JAPAN, America was involved in Vietnam. One day, I was with some black soldiers at the Yokota Air Force Base outside Tokyo. There were Japanese people demonstrating outside the base against the American presence in Vietnam. People were shouting, "Yankee, go home!" One of the soldiers commented, with a lonely expression on his face, "If I can, I *want* to go home."

I remember thinking that America had only white and black soldiers; I had never seen an Indian soldier. Moreover, I found out later that most Americans had not, either. When I came to the Navajo Indian Reservation in 1974, I discovered that the American Indians fought in World War I, World War II, and the Korean and Vietnam conflicts. It was a surprise. When I visited the Vietnam Memorial, the "Wall," in Washington, D.C., I saw a bronze sculpture of soldiers: a white man, a black man, and a Hispanic man. I couldn't find a representation of an American Indian. Were the American Indians the forgotten Americans? Were they American citizens? These questions struck me.

They stayed with me until I met the Navajo code talkers one winter day in Window Rock, Arizona, two years after I had come to the Navajo Indian Reservation. They had been part of the United States Marine Corps, and they were impressive. They had used their own language,

ABOVE: *Preparing to march in a parade at Shiprock, New Mexico, 1989.*

OPPOSITE: *Johnnie Alfred displays the Purple Heart awarded to him for his war-time service.*

Navajo, as a secret code during World War II, in the South Pacific, where four hundred of them were on active duty. They were responsible for many victories during the war, as Japanese cryptographers could not break their "code." I didn't know this kind of Indian veteran existed or that America's victory in the South Pacific was aided by an Indian language. These were the Indians America ignored!

When I found out about this group, I was deeply impressed by them. That snowy day was the Navajo Tribal Chairman's inauguration day, and about fifteen code talkers were in attendance. Carl Gorman, whom I had met earlier, introduced me to his company of men. They each wore the Navajo code talker's uniform—a turquoise-colored cap, a gold Navajo shirt, well-pressed khaki-colored pants, shiny black shoes, a turquoise necklace, and other decorations—with pride. Many Navajo people were proud of them. I decided then to take photographs of the Navajo code talkers.

ABOVE: *Marching in a Washington, D.C., parade, 1983.*

RIGHT: *A group of Navajo code talkers share an amusing moment in Washington, D.C., 1983.*

In 1982, I was made an honorary member and official association photographer. It felt somewhat strange, because my father was a survivor of the Japanese program of training men to be human torpedoes during the war in the South Pacific; these soldiers had been my father's enemies at one time. It

was awkward in a way, and I would never have expected to receive this kind of honor in America. Since then, I have traveled to Washington, D.C.; San Diego, California; Phoenix, Arizona; and other places with the code talkers and have taken picture after picture. I also started thinking about a book that would record these heroes.

In the beginning, I took photographs of them wearing their uniforms, but soon felt that I needed to go beyond that, with a more personal approach. I needed to visit and photograph them in their homes, a task that was made very difficult by the size of the Navajo Reservation (approximately the size of the state of West Virginia). These men were scattered across this vast land, and most of them had no telephones.

ABOVE: *Paul H. Blatchford (left), and Jack Morgan (right), review a newspaper article about their group; photograph taken San Diego, California, 1988.*

I decided to start by looking for their homes; when I located them, I asked if I could take photographs. If they were not at home, I had to go back again and again until I got what I needed. I found many of the men and their families, but there were others I simply could not reach. However, when I told them about my project, everyone was supportive and cooperated with me. Many were glad to see me, and welcomed my visits.

I would like to share some of the experiences I had with these men. When I first met Johnnie Alfred (Tuba City, Arizona), he showed me a Japanese soldier's razor that he had picked up almost a half-century ago on a South Pacific island; he had carefully put it away. When I visited his home, he gave it to me to "return to the Japanese." He said it was brand-new when he picked it up, but had rusted over the years. My heart was warmed by his goodwill.

Teddy Draper Sr. (Chinle, Arizona) went to Miyazaki, Japan, after the war was over as part of the occupation force. While there, he attended a Japanese-language school and remembered a lot of the language. He told me, "When I was going to boarding school, the U.S. government told us not to speak Navajo, but during the war, they *wanted* us to speak it!" He recalled thinking that "if I can get back to the reservation safely, I want to become a Navajo language teacher and educate young Navajos." He did return to his home and became a teacher.

ABOVE: *Shiprock, New Mexico, 1989, (left to right), Harold Y. Foster, Samuel Tso, and John Kinsel Sr.*

King Paul Mike Sr. (Kayenta, Arizona) had many Japanese souvenirs, including a rifle, paper money, and a flag from Okinawa. I saw that his name had been written in Japanese on the flag.

Lanabah Belone's husband, Harry Belone (Mexican Spring, New Mexico), passed away three years ago, and today, Mrs. Belone spends many of her days herding sheep and thinking about him. She showed me the uniform that he wore when he came back from San Diego in the forties. She told me that after he went to war, she supported their family by weaving and selling her rugs. When the children cried for their father, she cried with them, many times. She told me a lot in her own language.

David Jordan (Sweetwater, Arizona) lived an hour away from the paved highway, and it was hard to find his home. He used his tractor to fix the dirt road that had been washed away by rain a few days before I was scheduled to visit him. He did this just for me, and I was deeply moved. I got lost several times on the way to his house, and thought of giving up; when I found out how much trouble he'd gone to with the road, I was glad I'd persevered.

Carl Gorman (Fort Defiance, Arizona) was the first Navajo code talker I met. He had lied about his age to join the Marines in 1942—he was technically too old to go to war. Today, at eighty-two, he is the oldest Code Talker. He loves Japanese food and hopes to go to Japan someday. A former president of the Navajo Code Talkers Association, Mr. Gorman and his wife Mary (a former secretary) act as an information center for my project. I appreciate them very much.

When I started this project, I decided it was important to record as many as I could find. Although only about seventy-five photographs could be included in this book, there are about two hundred to two hundred fifty living code talkers. I regret that I could not visit all of them.

Many soldiers and their families spent time with me so that I could hear their experiences; I am grateful for the time they were willing to spend in front of my camera. I am also very happy to have my wife Ruth's love and cooperation in accomplishing this project; thank you, Ruth.

This book is dedicated to the Navajo code talkers, who defended their country by speaking their own language.

Kenji Kawano, Photographer
Window Rock, Arizona

INTRODUCTION

ON EACH OF THE ISLANDS of the Pacific where Marines stormed ashore in World War II, once the Americans gained a beachhead and moved inland, the Japanese defenders heard a "strange language, gurgling" through the headsets of their radio-listening equipment, which they were using to intercept American transmissions. They heard a code they could not decipher; it was difficult for the Japanese, as well as anyone else listening to these voice messages, to determine just what they *were* hearing. It was a language with Asian overtones and what seemed to be a lot of American double-talk. In fact, what they were intercepting were messages conveyed in an American Indian language, Navajo, a special kind of Navajo, at that.

One of the most significant needs in a combat situation is communications security, especially when troops were spread over a wide area and voice communication was the only certain method of maintaining contact. This being the case, military commanders and cryptologists long sought a perfect code, one which could not be broken under any circumstances. Even with the less-sophisticated equipment then in use, it was possible for Americans to break codes used by the Japanese military; it was hoped that they were unable to break ours, but of course, they could.

However, Navajo was one of the world's "hidden languages" in the sense that, at the time, it had no written form and no alphabet or other symbols. Complicating this situation even more were the facts that, first, the Navajo tongue was confined to the land of the Navajo Nation in the American Southwest, and second, there were dialect variations among the clans, and sometimes, within the clans themselves. Finally, only a handful of non-Navajos—usually anthropologists or missionaries—could speak the language.

ABOVE: *Bronze Star, awarded for valor under fire.*

OPPOSITE: *Bougainville, December 1943 (left to right, front row), Pvt.s Earl Johnny, Kee Etsicitty, John V. Goodluck, and Pfc. David Jordan; (back row), Pvt.s Jack C. Morgan, George H. Kirk, Tom H. Jones, and Cpl. Henry Bake Jr.*
PHOTOGRAPH COURTESY U.S. MARINE CORPS, NO. 69896.

One such Anglo (as Navajos describe people of European background) was Philip Johnston, a missionary's son raised on the Navajo Reservation who, from an early age, had Navajo playmates. He learned to speak fluent Navajo and, in addition, learned Navajo culture and traditions. When he was nine, he traveled with his father and two Navajo leaders to Washington, D.C., to meet with President Theodore Roosevelt to plead for fair treatment of the Navajo and Hopi by the American government. At this meeting, young Philip acted as translator.

ABOVE: *Colonel James G. Smith, signal officer for the First Marine Division, commends a group of New Mexican Navajo Indians who played an important role in maintaining communications during the Peleliu campaign. (Left to right, front row) Pfc. James T. Nahkai, Pfc. John H. Bowman, Pfc. Ira Manuelito, Pfc. Jimmy King, Pfc. Andrew Calleditto, Pfc. Lloyd Betone, Cpl. Lloyd Oliver, (back row): Pfc. Preston Toledo, Cpl. John Chee, Pfc. Sandy Burr, Pfc. Ben Manuelito, Pfc. Don Bahiya, Pfc. Edward Leuppe, brothers Pfc. Del Cayedito and Pfc. Ralph Cayedito.*
PHOTOGRAPH COURTESY U.S. MARINE CORPS, NO. 101511.

RIGHT: *Navajo Marine using walkie-talkie on a South Pacific beach, 1943.*
PHOTOGRAPH COURTESY U.S. MARINE CORPS, NO. 64081.

Mr. Johnston served in World War I and returned to California to study for a degree in Civil Engineering; he then went to work for the city of Los Angeles, meanwhile giving lectures about the Navajo and his early life with them. Shortly after the war with Japan commenced, he learned of an attempt by the military to develop some sort of code using its American Indian personnel as signalmen. Similar attempts had been made during World War I, but had never been successful because there were no equivalents for military terms in these languages. Mr. Johnson conceived of using Navajo to build a group of words that would be codes themselves.

In February 1942, at Camp Elliott (slightly north of San Diego), Mr. Johnston met with Marine Lieutenant Colonel James E. Jones, Area Signal Officer of Amphibious Corps, Pacific Fleet, headed by Major General Clayton B. Vogel. He told Colonel Jones that he

believed that the use by the Marine Corps of Navajo as a code language in voice (radio and wire) transmission could guarantee communications security. With the cooperation of four Navajos residing in the Los Angeles area, and another who was serving with the Navy in San Diego, Mr. Johnston presented a practical demonstration of his theory to General Vogel and his staff at Camp Elliott on 28 February.

Also present at the demonstration was Colonel Wethered Woodward, a member of the Divisions of Plans and Policies, the staff agency at the Washington headquarters of the U.S. Marine Corps, which would make the final decision to recruit the Navajo for any new cryptographic program. Colonel Woodward's first-hand observation of the demonstration later enabled him to fully support the establishment of the code-talker program.

Marine staff officers composed simulated field combat messages, which were handed to a Navajo man who then translated them into his language and transmitted to another Navajo on the other side of the line. The second Navajo translated them into English, in the same form in which they had been originally transmitted. Later, tests in the Pacific under combat conditions proved that classified messages could be translated into Navajo, transmitted, received, and translated back into English more quickly than messages which were encoded, transmitted, and decoded employing conventional cryptographic facilities and techniques.

The successful demonstration validated Mr. Johnston's claims and led General Vogel to recommend recruitment of two hundred Navajo Indians into the Marine Corps. They would be called "code talkers." The Commandant of the Marine Corps approved General Vogel's recommendation but limited the initial number of recruits to thirty (the actual number of

ABOVE: *Purple Heart, awarded for injuries sustained while in combat.*

LEFT: *Navajo enlistees are sworn into the U.S. Marine Corps as Navajo code talkers at Fort Wingate, New Mexico, October 1942.*
PHOTOGRAPH COURTESY BUREAU OF INDIAN AFFAIRS/ MILTON SNOW COLLECTION, NAVAJO TRIBAL MUSEUM, WINDOW ROCK, ARIZONA.

that first group was twenty-nine). After this approval, Mr. Johnston requested that, even though he was overage, he be allowed to enlist to help supervise the Navajo Marines once they began their communications training. His request was approved and he was given a staff sergeant warrant and assigned to the program at Camp Pendleton. At the outset, the entire Navajo code-talker program was classified as top secret.

With the approval of the Navajo Tribal Council, the Marines began recruiting young Navajo men at Window Rock, Arizona, in May 1942. Several were younger than eighteen—in their enthusiasm, they lied about their ages. Each recruit was in good physical condition and was fluent in both English and Navajo. Although the recruitment of Navajo men was comparatively slow at the time the program was first established, Marine recruiting teams later set up a central office at Fort Wingate, New Mexico. By August 1943, a total of one hundred ninety-one Navajo men had joined the Marine Corps for assignment to the code talker program; an estimated three hundred seventy-five to four hundred twenty individuals eventually were involved. Many more young Navajo men volunteered to become code talkers than could be accepted, and an undetermined number served as regular Marines.

After they were signed up, the Navajo recruits underwent basic boot camp training at the San Diego Marine Corps Recruit Depot. Following boot camp, they were sent to the Field Signal Battalion Training Center at Camp Pendleton in Oceanside, California.

Boot camp is usually a traumatic experience for any Marine recruit, and it must have been even more so for these young Navajo men, most of whom had never been off tribal land (the Navajo Reservation occupies approximately seventeen million acres of land in Arizona, New Mexico, and Utah) or traveled by train or undergone the type of training they received at the hands of Marine drill instructors. It was equally challenging for the non-Navajo instructors to instruct these recruits in basic military skills; some of the Anglo drill instructors had difficulty in coping with Navajo imperturbability.

ABOVE AND RIGHT: *Campaign ribbons and medals received by Preston Toledo.*

ABOVE: *Second all-Navajo platoon at San Diego, California, 1943.*

Initially, the course at Camp Pendleton consisted of one hundred seventy-six hours of instruction in basic communications procedures and equipment, over a period of four weeks. The syllabus contained courses in subjects such as printing and message writing, the Navajo vocabulary, voice procedure, Navajo message transmission, wire laying, pole climbing, and organization of a Marine infantry regiment, among other things. At the same time, the first group of recruits devised Navajo words for military terms which were not part of their language: Navajo clan names were given to the different Marine Corps units; names of birds (*chicken hawk*) denoted airplanes; the commanding general was *war chief* and a major general was *two star*. Alternate terms were provided in the code for letters frequently repeated in the English language. For example, each letter of the alphabet was given three different forms: *ant, ax,* and *apple* were the forms of the letter A. For B, the words were *badger, bear,* and *barrel,* and so on for the rest of the alphabet. To compound the difficulty, all code talkers had to memorize both primary and alternate code terms, for while the basic material was printed for use in training in the United States, the vocabulary lists could not be carried in a combat area for fear of them falling into enemy hands and compromising the whole program.

Once the code talkers completed training at Camp Pendleton, they were sent to the Pacific for assignment to Marine combat units already deployed. Major General Alexander A. Vandergrift, commanding general of the 1st Marine Division, which had landed on Guadalcanal on 7 August 1942, was so pleased with the performance of the Navajo code talkers during the campaign that at the end of the operation in December,

ABOVE: *Cpl. Henry Bake Jr., Fort Defiance, Arizona (right), and Pfc. George H. Kirk, Leupp, Arizona (left), operate a portable radio set in the Bougainville jungle, December 1943.*
PHOTOGRAPH COURTESY U.S. MARINE CORPS, NO. 69889-B.

OPPOSITE: *Pfc. Preston Toledo (left), and Pfc. Frank Toledo (right), cousins attached to a Marine Artillery Regiment in the South Pacific, relay orders in Navajo over a field radio, July 1943.*
PHOTOGRAPH COURTESY U.S. MARINE CORPS, NO. 57875.

he sent a message to the Commandant of the Marine Corps requesting assignment of eighty-three more to the division. In May 1943, in response to a request by the Commandant to his combat commanders for

information on the progress and success of the program, the various divisions reported that excellent results had been achieved to that date in the employment of the code talkers in training and combat situations, and that they had performed in a highly commendable fashion.

This praise continued throughout the war and came from commanders at all

ABOVE: *Marine radio messengers (left to right) Pfc. Joe Hosteen Kelwood, Steamboat Canyon, Ganado, Arizona; Pvt. Floyd Saupitty, Lawton, Oklahoma; and Pfc. Alex Williams, Red Lake, Leupp, Arizona, at Okinawa, March 1945. Williams and Kelwood were veterans of Peleliu.*
PHOTOGRAPH COURTESY U.S. MARINE CORPS, NO. 129851.

RIGHT: *Navajo code talkers (left to right) Pfc. Edmond John, Shiprock, New Mexico; Pfc. Wilsie H. Bitsie, Mexican Springs, New Mexico; and Pfc. Eugene R. Crawford, Chinle, Arizona; August 1943, Noumea.*
PHOTOGRAPH COURTESY U.S. MARINE CORPS, NO. 61431.

levels. At the same time, senior Marines in the Pacific Theatre recommended the distribution of code talkers throughout the combat units: two per each infantry and artillery battalion; four per each infantry and artillery regiment; and so on. The commanders also recommended that the

primary duty of the Navajo Marines was to be "talkers," transmitting messages over telephone and radio circuits. Their secondary duty was to act as message-center personnel (messengers). "This designation will not limit their usefulness to the Marine Corps, however, as they have shown remarkable aptitude in their performance as general-duty Marines," the commanders noted.

Following the Guam and Peleliu landings in 1944, Marine III Amphibious Corps reported that the use of code talkers in these two operations "was considered indispensable for the rapid transmission of classified dispatches. [Traditional] enciphering and deciphering time would have prevented vital operational information from being dispatched or delivered to staff sections with any degree of speed." Later, at Iwo Jima in 1945, the code talkers sent messages from the beachhead to division and corps commanders still afloat on the command ships off the beaches, and after the division commands landed, from division headquarters ashore to the corps commanders afloat.

By the end of the war, code talkers had been assigned to all six Marine divisions in the Pacific and to Marine Raider and parachute units as well. They took part in every Marine assault, from Guadalcanal in 1942 to Okinawa in 1945. In addition to the normal hazards of combat, the Navajo code talkers occasionally faced danger from their own side. At the outset, and as early as Guadalcanal, Marine commanders were concerned that the oriental-looking Navajo might be mistaken for Japanese. Toward the end of that campaign, an army unit picked up a code talker and sent a message to his Marine command advising that it had captured a Japanese in Marine utilities and wearing Marine identification tags. A Marine officer was sent to see if the prisoner was indeed a Japanese soldier and was startled to find that he was a Navajo code talker. Other cases of mistaken identity occurred, especially when army units fought alongside Marines, inasmuch as these soldiers knew nothing about the Navajo.

ABOVE: *Pfc. George H. Kirk, Ganado, Arizona (left), and Pfc. John V. Goodluck, Lukachukai, Arizona (right), in Guam.*
PHOTOGRAPH COURTESY U.S. MARINE CORPS, NO. 94236.

During World War II, I served in the 1st Marine Division's Headquarters and Service Battalion and took part in the landings on Peleliu and Okinawa. One of the units in that battalion was the Division Signal Company, to which Navajo code talkers were assigned. I have a faint memory of Navajo Marines, but at the time had no idea of what they did. It wasn't until many years later that I learned of the service they performed in combat and how they were employed. I doubt that many other Marines, except other signalmen—Marine riflemen that the Navajos supported—and those who had a "need to know" were aware of the code talkers and their unique qualities.

It wasn't until July 1971, when I traveled to Window Rock, Arizona, capital of the Navajo Nation, to interview code talkers for the Marine Corps Oral History Program, that I learned more about these men. The code talkers had not been nationally recognized until 1969, when the

ABOVE: *Pfc. Samual Sandoval, radio operator, relaxes under a tori gate in a former Japanese park, surveying Okinawa Shima, April 1945.*
PHOTOGRAPH COURTESY U.S. MARINE CORPS, NO. 128883.

4th Marine Division Association held its reunion in Chicago. At that time, a group of code talkers was invited to the reunion and presented with a medallion specially minted in commemoration of their services. Lee Cannon, a member of the 4th Division Association, was largely instrumental in having the code talkers recognized.

Not long after this 1969 event, Philip Johnston presented his code talker–related papers to the Navajo Tribal Museum in Window Rock. In 1970, Martin Link, curator of the museum, showed the papers to Dr. C. Gregory Crampton and to other members of the staff of the Doris Duke Indian Oral History Project at the University of Utah. At that time, it was strongly recommended that the experiences of the code talkers be captured on tape and added to the museum's archives. Plans were then formulated to bring together surviving code talkers to their first reunion; this took place at Window Rock in July 1971. It was to this gathering that I was sent to collect interviews.

Also present were Dr. Crampton and his interviewers and Doris A.

Paul, who was conducting research for her book, *The Navajo Code Talkers*, which was later published. Window Rock and the Navajo people were an entirely new experience for me, for not only had I no real knowledge of or association with Native Americans, it was the first time I had ever been in an environment such as that in Arizona. It was an exciting and interesting experience, for I saw that the Navajo were a beautiful and proud people who cherished and relished their traditions and customs despite the many years of effort on the part of the American government to direct them into Anglo ways. Together, Mrs. Paul, Dr. Crampton, and I interviewed a large number of the veterans and were present for the ceremonies surrounding this first code talker reunion.

It was more than apparent that, despite the passage of twenty-five years or more since they had last been in uniform, these former code talkers were still strongly partisan Marines. More importantly, the patriotism of these men was as steadfast, if not more so, as when they first joined the Marine Corps at their country's request. In recognition of their dedicated service to America during World War II, the Navajo code talkers were awarded a Certificate of Appreciation by the President of the United States in December 1971. It recognized the fact that their unique achievements constituted a proud chapter in the history of the United States Marine Corps. The President further stated that "their patriotism, resourcefulness, and courage have earned them the gratitude of all Americans."

The heritage of service and loyalty that they established in World War II is, in many cases, carried on by their sons and grandsons who are now Marines. These young Navajo Marines are charged with the responsibility of carrying on that tradition, sensitively chronicled in this book by Kenji Kawano.

ABOVE: *World War II Victory medal.*

Benis M. Frank, Head
Marine Corps Oral History Program
Marine Corps History and Museums Division

THE PHOTOGRAPHS

"The war was very sad. I saw dead Marines on the beach
at Iwo Jima...we had to go through them."

DAN AKEE
Kin Yaa'aanii Clan

4th Marine Division
KWAJALEIN
SAIPAN
TINIAN
IWO JIMA

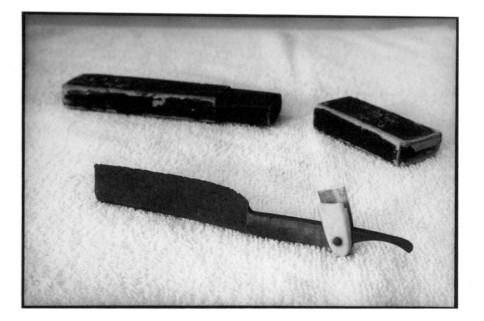

Code talker Johnnie Alfred of Tuba City, Arizona, picked up this Japanese soldier's razor almost a half-century ago on a South Pacific island.

*"All I can say is that
I was just lucky."*

JOHNNIE ALFRED
Todich'ii'nii Clan

6th Marine Division
TARAWA
SAIPAN
OKINAWA
TINIAN
KYUKYU ISLANDS
MARIANA ISLANDS

"When I volunteered, I never thought about getting hurt. I was discharged August 3, 1947, and was awarded a Purple Heart and the South Pacific ribbons."

EDWARD B. ANDERSON JR.
Honaghaabnii Clan

1st Marine Division
AUSTRALIA
NEW GUINEA

BENNY ARVISO
Tsi'naajinii Clan

1st Marine Division
HAWAII
GUADALCANAL
SOLOMON ISLANDS
OKINAWA

"These stories I don't care to relate."

LEWIS F. AYZE
Tachii'nii and Todich'ii'nii Clans

3rd Marine Division
HAWAII
SAIPAN
GUAM

*"One of my friends was in the
same [fox]hole as I was; he was
a Mormon from Salt Lake City,
Utah. He gave me his parent's
address and a note to send to
them if he got shot."*

SIDNEY BEDONI
Todich'ii'nii Clan

2nd, 4th, 5th Marine Divisions
NEW CALEDONIA
BRITISH SOLOMON ISLANDS
SAIPAN
OKINAWA
RYUKYUIS ISLAND
GUADALCANAL
IWO JIMA

FLEMING D. BEGAY SR.
To dich'ii'nii Clan

2nd Marine Division
GUADALCANAL
AUSTRALIA
NEW ZEALAND
GILBERT ISLANDS
TARAWA
MARSHALL ISLANDS

"I was eighteen years old…I can't recall [exactly] what I did all those years, but it was quite an experience."

"I was with the halftrack crew; instead of going to the beach, we hit the pier. The halftrack blew up and a lot of guys were killed. Instead of fighting, I helped those who were floating around back to safety. When I got to the beach, there were a lot of dead and dying Marines lying there. On the third day, I was shot. The next day, I was on a [hospital] ship."

JERRY C. BEGAY SR.
Kinlichii'nii Clan
2nd Marine Division
TARAWA

"At Guadalcanal, in August 1942, I was never so scared in my entire life. I didn't know if I was going to make it or not... I wasn't at all sure that I was going to make it."

Jimmy Begay and his grandson
Scott Begay, four.

JIMMY BEGAY
Naasht'ezhi dine's Clan

1st, 3rd Marine Divisions
GUADALCANAL
TAIWAN
OKINAWA

*"I was in combat training in Okinawa...rough days,
rough nights. I was eighteen years old."*

LEE H. BEGAY
Naashgalidine's Clan

2nd Marine Division
OKINAWA
IWO JIMA

"We were disciplined...I learned to survive combat. The first hour, I was with my radio, communicating with other floats. I was scared, very scared; mortars and artillery were landing everywhere, but I wasn't hit. The Iwo Jima sand was ashy and hard to walk on, but I had to carry my radio and other equipment across it. I was sent to replace Pfc. Paul Kinlacheeny, who was killed on the beach.

"I was awarded six battle stars during my military career for being in major battles from Iwo Jima to the Korean War. I was never wounded or shot but was missed by inches, and missed being captured by thirty minutes or less. I was very lucky to have gotten through that time. Maybe because I believe in the traditional Navajo ways and felt that the Great Spirit was protecting me. My parents, both very traditional Navajos, had ceremonies for me using clothes that I had worn before I left home to go in the service. These ceremonies protected my well-being, so I could survive."

THOMAS H. BEGAY
Tsi'najinii and Ashiihi Clans

5th Marine Division
HAWAII
ENEWETAK ATOLL
GUAM
TINIAN
SAIPAN
IWO JIMA

"We went to the front lines, most of the time carrying the radio, talking in our own language."

WILMER BELINDA

1st Marine Division
OKINAWA

Mrs. Belone recalls: *"I supported my family by weaving rugs when my husband went to the war. He was a very warm, caring person."*

Mrs. Harry Belone Sr. with the service photograph of her husband.

HARRY BELONE SR.
Tachii'nii and Tsi'naajinii Clans

1st Marine Division
GUADALCANAL
GUAM
IWO JIMA

"I was drafted. When I finished boot camp, I was told they had a special job for me. I didn't know what it could be, but soon found out it was as a code talker."

HARRY BENALLY

1st Marine Division
OKINAWA

Mrs. Benally recalls: *"He said to me one day, 'Nobody realizes what we had to go through. It was just terrible.' He never watched war movies."*

Mrs. Johnny Ashi Benally and her granddaughter Brooke Benally, eleven, with the service photograph of her husband.

JOHNNY BENALLY
Maiideeshgiizhiini and Kin yaa'aanii Clans

1st, 3rd, 5th Marine Divisions
SOUTHWEST AND
CENTRAL PACIFIC

HOWARD BILLIMAN JR.

Kin yaa'aanii Clan

2nd Marine Division
NEW ZEALAND
TARAWA
SAIPAN
TINIAN
OKINAWA

"I was an instructor at Camp Pendleton; a lot of Navajo boys went through camp there and then went overseas. At Tarawa, we had a hard time...men were getting killed right and left...I was scared."

"Why did I kill? This has had great psychological bearing on me, and still does."

WILSIE H. BITSIE
Bit'aa'nii and Zuni Tachii'nii Clans

1st, 2nd Marine Divisions
MIDWAY ISLANDS
MAKIN
NEW CALEDONIA
GUAM
EMARU
AUKLAND ISLANDS
WELLINGTON

"On Iwo Jima, about six days after the landing, I had a humorous experience. We had moved our front line about two hundred yards forward. Three of us were in a foxhole when the Japanese stopped shooting. Privates Raymond Smith and Ambrose Howard told me to sit down and go to sleep. I tried, but I couldn't. Suddenly, flares were shot over the Japanese line and a shadow of a tall tombstone was moving back and forth. We thought the Japanese were coming and we started shooting, until someone yelled for us to stop before the Japanese found our location.

"About an hour later, when everything was quiet again, Howard said he'd try to get some sleep; he squatted down and within a few minutes he yelled! Smith and I didn't know what was wrong; Smith shined the flashlight on the back of Howard's neck. We saw a sand crab pinching him...he said he thought a Japanese soldier had got hold of him!"

PAUL H. BLATCHFORD
Hashtl'ishnii Clan

5th Marine Division
SOLOMON ISLANDS
GUAM
SAIPAN
TINIAN
IWO JIMA

"Early in 1943, a Japanese soldier almost shot me in the head while I was patrolling for snipers after the island [Saipan] was secure. Bullets started flying, and I got behind a tree. I was curious to see where they were coming from. A bullet struck the tree about four inches from my head."

JOHN BROWN JR.
Ma'iideeshgiizhinii and Tachii'nii Clans

2nd Marine Division
GUADALCANAL
SAIPAN
TINIAN
TARAWA

"I was drafted in 1945 and went to code-talker's school for eight months. Then, when I was ready to board a ship for the South Pacific, the war ended."

SAM CHARLIE SR.
Nat'ch dine's Clan

THOMAS CLAW
Ta'neezahnii Clan

1st Marine Division
NEW CALEDONIA
AUSTRALIA
NEW GUINEA
PAVUVU AND RUSSEL ISLANDS
PELILUI AND PALAU ISLANDS
GUADALCANAL
ULITHI
OKINAWA

*"One night, on Okinawa, I volunteered for the security line for
our bivoac area. Everything went fine until early morning when a
Japanese soldier surprised us with a hand grenade. Three of us were
wounded; two were evacuated to a Naval hospital that same morning
[June 23, 1945]."*

"The war dogs come to mind. They were used in the fields, and would bark in the night when the enemy was coming. When the dogs barked, we knew they were nearby; we'd shoot flares so that we could see them, and then would shoot. That's what I remember about the war."

BOB ETSITTY CRAIG
Bitaa'nii and Tachii'nii Clans

3rd Marine Division
IWO JIMA

EUGENE R. CRAWFORD
Naanesht'ezhi tachiini Clan

1st Marine Division
SOLOMON ISLANDS
OKINAWA
IWO JIMA

"At one point during, I was captured by U.S. Army soldiers, who thought I was Japanese."

"I participated in the bloody battle of Iwo Jima on February 19, 1945. They told us to secure communications and telephone wire under combat conditions on the island within three days, but it took about a month."

TEDDY DRAPER SR.
Ashiihi Clan

5th, 28th Marine Divisions
HAWAII
MARSHALL ISLANDS
GUAM
IWO JIMA
SASEBO
KAGOSHIMA
MIYAZAKI

"I was a messenger sentry and did occupation-force work on Kushu Island [Japan] for about a year and a half."

Harold Evans and his wife, Vinginie.

HAROLD EVANS
To dich'ii'nii Clan
2nd Marine Division
OKINAWA
SAIPAN

*"I was seventeen and in high school at Fort Wingate in 1942;
I wanted to protect my country. For thirty-two days, I was
radio war chief at Iwo Jima. If I had the chance, I'd like to
go back to some of the islands I was on during the war."*

HAROLD Y. FOSTER
Dziltl'klanii Clan

2nd, 5th Marine Divisions
GILBERT ISLANDS
IWO JIMA
NAGASAKI
SASEBO

"On post guard duty one night, six of us were sharing one foxhole when we heard something coming at us through the underbrush. We opened fire...it was a wild pig!"

John V. Goodluck and his wife.

JOHN GOODLUCK
To'aheedliinii and Dibe lizhini Clans

3rd Marine Division
GUADALCANAL
BOUGAINVILLE
GUAM
IWO JIMA

"I was in sick bay at Pearl Harbor and thought I was going to die."

CARL NELSON GORMAN
Dibe lizhini Clan

2nd Marine Division
GUADALCANAL
TARAWA
SAIPAN
TINIAN

"One experience that stands out in my memory is being on combat patrol in Okinawa; our patrol was pinned down for two days — the antenna of my radio was shot off, but I was able to get a message through [in code] for reinforcements."

ROY O. HAWTHORNE
Kin lichii'nii Clan

1st Marine Division
GUADALCANAL
OKINAWA
GUAM
MIDWAY ISLANDS
JAPAN
CHINA

Navajo code talkers pay respect to one of America's most famous Indian soldiers, Ira Hayes, at Arlington National Cemetery, Arlington, Virginia.

"A week after landing on the shores of Saipan during World War II, a fellow Navajo code talker and I were in a prone position, discussing the fact that we didn't have a chance if we moved. I put my helmet [on my rifle] and raised it out of the foxhole, and shots sprayed across our position, mostly from our right. The Army had taken the right flank. It was the first time these soldiers had been where actual fighting was going on and they were shooting at anything and everything.

"The Japanese were on our left; the possibility of being shot by them was also very real. We stayed down, waiting. The shouts and screams of fellow soldiers were all around us, and we thought these were our last minutes on earth. Suddenly, I heard a deep 'THUMP' next to me, where my fellow code talker was lying, and I was scared I would be next. It took every ounce of courage I had to look over at him—I expected blood and guts. To my relief—and the relief of my foxhole partner—I saw one of the biggest bullfrogs I'd ever seen on my partner's back."

SAMUEL TOM HOLIDAY
Todich'ii'nii Clan

4th Marine Division
SAIPAN
IWO JIMA
MARSHALL ISLANDS
TINIAN

DENNIE HOUSTEEN
Tachii'nii Clan

3rd Marine Division
BOUGAINVILLE
GUAM
IWO JIMA
NEW ZEALAND
GUADALCANAL

"When I was going to school in Ganado, Arizona, one of the original twenty-nine code talkers, James Manuelito, came to our school wearing his Marine blues. He looked great—I really liked the uniform, and it made me want to join the Marines. I was the only one from that school to go into the Marines, but I never had a chance to wear the dress blues."

"What I remember is carrying messages from headquarters to the front line, night and day, for eighty-two days. I lost friends in Okinawa. When I came home from the war, my family had two-day and two-night healing ceremonies, as well as two squaw dances, to help me get well, but I am still sick."

DESWOOD R. JOHNSON SR.

6th Marine Division
OKINAWA

"It was two or three days after we hit the island in Bougainville that our sargeant told me to go to the rear where the command post was. I got lost, and it began to get dark. An Army security guard shoved his gun in my back and took my rifle away because he thought I was Japanese. I told him who I was and that I was looking for the message center. He took me to camp headquarters, where another Navajo soldier recognized me. I was freed after that."

DAVID JORDAN
Bit'aa'nii Clan

3rd Marine Division
BOUGAINVILLE
SOLOMON ISLANDS
IWO JIMA

WILSON KEEDAH SR.
Kin yaa'aanii Clan

6th Marine Division
OKINAWA
GUADALCANAL
IWO JIMA

"I went to war because there were no jobs on the reservation."

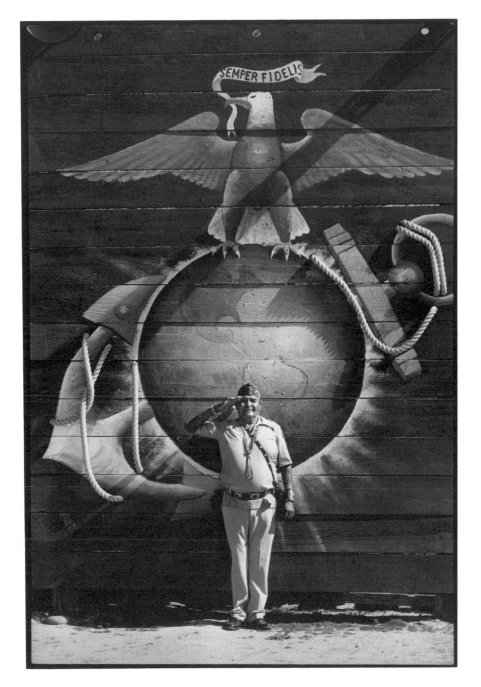

JOE H. KELLWOOD

1st Marine Division

"Throughout the war against the Japanese in the Pacific, we code talkers had to brush up on our codes at every opportunity. When the fighting got bad, words would fail us for a second; it was a good thing we [Navajos] have so many sounds in our language."

WILLIAM KIEN
Kin yaa'aanii Clan

4th Marine Division
MARSHALL ISLANDS
SAIPAN
TINIAN
IWO JIMA

*"While I was stationed in Guam, I saw a soldier step on a
landmine. Both of his legs and one hand were destroyed.
He asked for a smoke, saying 'I still have one hand.'"*

JOHN KINSEL SR.
Kin lichii'nii Clan

3rd Marine Division
GUADALCANAL
BOUGAINVILLE
GUAM
IWO JIMA

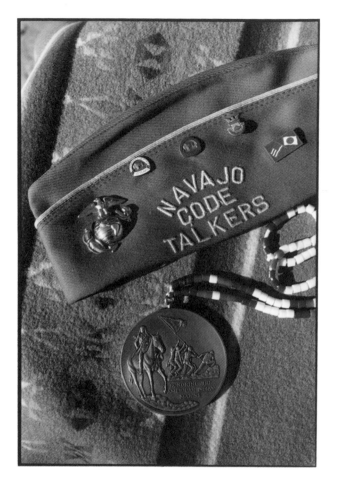

*The Navajo code talkers wear
their insignia with pride.*

"*The Japanese were preparing to attack an American installation on Guam. Our Marine reconnaissance found their location and the code talkers sent a message to a battleship and two artillery units to tell them where the target was. The Japanese were wiped out and our commander, Major General Erikine, was saved by our language.*"

GEORGE H. KIRK SR.
Ta'neezahnii Clan

3rd Marine Division

NEW CALEDONIA	MARIANA ISLANDS
GUADALCANAL	JOHNSTON ISLANDS
BOUGAINVILLE	IWO JIMA
NEW GUINEA	
MARSHALL ISLANDS	
ENEWETAK ATOLL	
GUAM	

"While on the hospital ship Benevolence, my friend and I took liberty and went into the village of Yokusuka, which was supposed to be off-limits to American soldiers. We came back okay, and met some nice people in the village."

Mike Kiyaani and his wife.

MIKE KIYAANI
Ashiihi Clan

6th Marine Division
GUADALCANAL
GUAM
OKINAWA

"I wanted to join the Marines very much, but I couldn't make the weight requirement. So I ate bananas, hoping to gain weight. Even though I wasn't quite heavy enough, they took me in."

REX T. KONTZ
To dikozi Clan

Mrs. Alene Kontz holding the service photograph of her husband Rex
(deceased February 12, 1980).

"During a lull in the battle for the Roi-Namur atolls in the Marshall Islands, our outfit was pulled off the front lines for some rest. The battalion command post was set up in a shell crater adjacent to a steel-reinforced concrete building. The men in the platoon were lazily enjoying this brief rest period when someone noticed that the heavy steel door of the building was very cautiously and slowly opening. Most of the guys trained their carbines on the door. Out came a Japanese, naked except for what looked like a g-string, with his hands in the air.

"The platoon leader immediately ordered everyone to hold their fire, but apparently some trigger-happy Marine didn't get the word and took a pot-shot at the poor guy. Then twenty or more carbines blazed away. The Japanese took off and saved himself by diving into a shell hole.

"With all of the shooting going on, the platoon leader was shouting 'Cease fire. And goddam, if you can't hit the bastard, leave him alone!' Suddenly, all the shooting stopped.

"Horrified at the poor marksmanship exhibited by the men in his platoon, the platoon leader unmercifully derided everyone. 'What kind of Marines are you anyway, when you can't even scratch a target ten feet in front of you?' One shy Marine resolved the embarrassing situation for everyone by saying 'Sir, I was only shooting at the man's head.' The rest of the men agreed that they, too, were aiming in that direction.

"The Japanese was coaxed out of the shell hole, given food and clothing, treated, and escorted to the rear. He was none the worse physically, except for a few minor scratches sustained in his desperate dive into the shell hole."

KEITH M. LITTLE
Todich'ii'nii Clan

4th Marine Division
ROI-NAMUR
MARSHALL ISLANDS
SAIPAN
TINIAN
MARIANA ISLANDS
IWO JIMA

KING PAUL MIKE SR.
Totsohnii Clan

6th Marine Division
GUADALCANAL
GUAM
OKINAWA
TAIWAN

"I was with a Regimental Intelligence section; we were told not to claim that we were a code talker [if we were captured]. At Guadalcanal I was put on a speedboat to look for Japanese airplanes. We were spotted and shot at a couple of times."

"At Guam, I was on night guard and almost got shot. My friend from Shiprock [New Mexico] was later killed on the [battle] field."

JACK C. MORGAN
To'baazhni'azhi Clan

3rd Marine Division
GUAM
IWO JIMA
BOUGAINVILLE

*"On the beach at Palua Island,
a landmine exploded about
six feet from our radio post.
It killed a lot of Marines,
and blew both the dead
and living into the foxholes."*

JAMES T. NAHKAI JR.
*Hask'aa hadzoho and
Naakaii dine's Clans*

1st Marine Division

NEW CALEDONIA	SOLOMON ISLANDS
NEW GUINEA	PALUA ISLANDS
NEW BRITIAN	OKINAWA
AUSTRALIA	CHINA

"Getting back home alive was my major goal."

HARDING NEGALE
Tabaaha Clan

6th Marine Division
GUADALCANAL
OKINAWA
GUAM
MANILA

HOWARD HOSTEEN NEZ SR.
Naakiidine's and Tabaaha Clans

3rd Marine Division
GUAM
NEW CALEDONIA
MARSHALL ISLANDS
GUADALCANAL
CHRISTMAS ISLAND

"I was a code talker, also a scout and a sniper. I was shot in the leg in Guam, and a field nurse picked me up and dragged me out of the battle. I was sent to a hospital in Hawaii, where I stayed for six months, and then was sent home in 1944. I couldn't work when I came back, but went to both a medicineman and a doctor and am okay now."

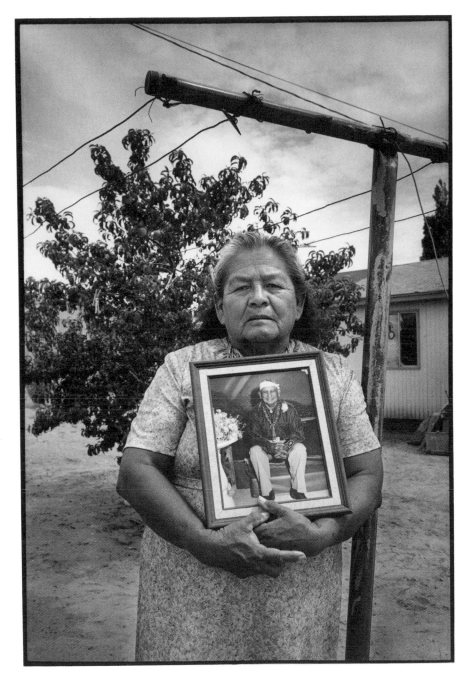

SIDNEY NEZ

Mrs. Sidney Nez
holding a photograph
of her husband.

*"In Okinawa, I was almost shot
by soldiers on my own side,
who mistook me for the enemy
when I came out of a cave.
One of my white buddies came
out just in time to save me."*

ROY NOTAH
To dich'ii'nii Clan

3rd Amphibious Division
OKINAWA
GUAM
BOUGAINVILLE

"I was the lead man in a radio platoon in a forward echelon against hostile forces."

Mr. Oliver was awarded the Purple Heart, the Bronze Star, the Presidential Unit Citation, and the American Unit Citation, for his service in the Pacific Theatre.

WILLARD V. OLIVER
Bit'aa'nii and Kin lichii'nii Clans

2nd Marine Division

TARAWA
SAIPAN
TINIAN
OKINAWA
NAGASAKI

PAUL A. PARRISH
Todich'ii'nii Clan

1st Marine Division
GUADALCANAL
BOUGAINVILLE
GUAM
SAIPAN
IWO JIMA

Paul A. Parrish and his son.

"When I was inducted into the service, one of the commitments I made was that I was willing to die for my country — the U.S., the Navajo Nation, and my family. My [native] language was my weapon."

DAVID E. PATTERSON
Tachii'nii and Kinlichii'nii Clans

4th Marine Division
ROI ATOLL
MARSHALL ISLANDS
KWAJALEIN ATOLL

"I liked the Marines…they gave me basic training, good food, and a scholarship. After I was discharged, I was able to go to school."

N.M. State Senator John Pinto

JOHN PINTO
Dibe lizhini and Tachii'nii Clans

"I saw the American flag raised on Mt. Suribachi…we cheered and jumped around when it went up. After World War II ended, I stayed in the Marines, got married, and went to school at Quantico, Virginia, and San Diego, California, in electronics. I served in Korea, in the Mediterranean, during the Cuban crisis, and Vietnam. Finally retired from the Marines in 1972."

WILLSON H. PRICE
Tabaaha Clan

1st, 2nd, 5th Marine Divisions

GUADALCANAL	OKINAWA
SOLOMON ISLANDS	SAIPAN
AUSTRALIA	JAPAN
NEW ZEALAND	CHINA
IWO JIMA	

"I remember the early hours of combat after landing on Iwo Jima; I and several others fell off the landing cargo net.... We got in the landing craft and circled the battleship, the Tennessee, *before we got ashore. Our landing craft was hit sideways and overturned and we lost our equipment. The* Tennessee *was firing over our heads and the Navy and Marine planes were bombing and strafing Mt. Suribachi. Some of the planes didn't make their dives and crashed into the mountain."*

Merril L. Sandoval and his grandson Lenard Dillon, six.

MERRIL L. SANDOVAL
*Naasht'exhi dine's, Tabaaha
and Naakaii dine's Clans*

2nd, 5th Marine Divisions
MARIANA ISLANDS   HAWAII
MARSHALL ISLANDS   MIDWAY ISLANDS
BONIN ISLANDS   IWO JIMA

SAMUEL F. SANDOVAL
Naasht'ezhi dine's Clan

1st Marine Division
GUADALCANAL
BOUGAINVILLE
GUAM
PALUA ISLANDS
ENEWETAK ATOLL
OKINAWA

"Navajos' main diet is mutton and goat meat. On Okinawa, we discovered a lot of domesticated goats running loose; their owners were behind the skirmishes and combat lines. Some of us [code talkers] captured and butchered a few of the animals and had a feast. The non-Navajo military men were surprised."

"I recall securing the beachhead on Saipan on June 15, 1944. Shells were raining down and fanatical Japanese soldiers used civilians as shields. The American flag was raised on Marpi Point on July 9, after twenty-five days of fighting; it was run up a Japanese telephone pole."

SAMMY SILVERSMITH
Hashtl'ishnii
and Naakaii Dine's Clans

4th Marine Division
MARSHALL ISLANDS
MARIANA ISLANDS
TINIAN
IWO JIMA
HAWAII

"My overseas duty assignment as part of the replacement force began with hard manual labor— transporting war material and supplies via ship and L.S.T. between Saipan and Okinawa. I also participated in radio communications operations."

ARCENIO SMILEY
*Tse nahabilnii and
Honaghaabnii Clans*
SAIPAN
ENEWETAK ATOLL
OKINAWA
KAGOSHIMA

"I walked the full length of Saipan and Tinian islands carrying maps and escorting replacements, prisoners, and farmers. At the same time, I operated the radio for the riflemen and was under fire myself while delivering messages."

ALBERT SMITH

4th, 14th, 23rd Marine Divisions
MARSHALL ISLANDS
SAIPAN
TINIAN
IWO JIMA

GEORGE SMITH

2nd Marine Division
SAIPAN
TINIAN

"I saw the raising of the flag on Mt. Suribachi."　　**RAYMOND R. SMITH**
Kin lichii'nii Clan

2nd, 5th Marine Divisions
IWO JIMA

JOHNNIE TABAHA SR.
Tabaaha and Honaghaabnii Clans

4th Marine Division
GUAM
GUADALCANAL

"I lost my dad while I was overseas, and that hurt the most.
Facing the enemy at Saipan and seeing my buddies
killed all around me was very bad."

FRANCIS T. THOMPSON
Honaghaahnii Clan

2nd, 8th Marine Divisions
SAIPAN
OKINAWA
NAGASAKI

FRANK T. THOMPSON
Honaghaabnii and Tachii'nii Clans

2nd Marine Division

NEW ZEALAND	PEARL HARBOR
NEW CALEDONIA	KWAJALEIN ATOLL
GUADALCANAL	SAIPAN
NEW HEBRIDES	TINIAN
TARAWA	ENEWETAK ATOLL
	ABEMAMA

"I recall the Tarawa Campaign and the explosion of our ship, a L.S.T., before the Saipan invasion. Every campaign had its own story."

*"I remember most my visit
to the Great Wall of China;
I thought at the time
'I can't believe I'm here.'"*

Frank Carl Todecheenie and his grandson
Lederrick Max Smith, four.

FRANK CARL TODECHEENIE
*Todich'iinii and
Hashk'aaha'zohi' Clans*

4th, 6th Marine Divisions
GUAM
PEARL HARBOR
NORTH CHINA
OKINAWA

BILL HENRY TOLEDO

Ta'neezahnii Clan

3rd Marine Division

NEW ZEALAND
GUADALCANAL
BOUGAINVILLE
GUAM
IWO JIMA

"I had a very close call on the fifth day after we landed on Guam in 1944. Our radio and telephone were knocked out. A sniper took several shots at me as I was delivering a message [as a runner] from the front line to regimental headquarters on the beach. I learned later that that sniper had been picking off Marines earlier in the day."

"I went to Fort Wingate to take the physical examination before joining the Marines. I weighed 119 pounds, and had to weigh 122 to be accepted; Frank Toledo told me to drink a lot of water. So I did and weighed in at 123."

Mr. Toledo received the Bronze Star, American Campaign Medal, Asiatic Pacific Campaign Medal, World War II Victory Medal, and the China Service Medal.

PRESTON TOLEDO
Todich'ii'nii Clan

1st Marine Division
AUSTRALIA
CAPE GLAUCESTER
PALONLS
NEW BRITIAN
OKINAWA
PEKING
CHINA

PAUL EDWARD TSO SR.
Naashgali Dine's and To dich'ii'nii Clans

6th Marine Division
GUAM
TSINGTAO

"I was afraid of nothing. I felt if I was going to end my life in war, that was the way it was to be."

"Early one morning I went to the top deck of our ship and looked left and right. As far as I could see there were ships and I thought to myself 'How can we lose this war?'"

SAMUEL N. TSO
Tachii'nii Clan

5th Marine Division
IWO JIMA
SASEBO
NAGASAKI

"My mother would not let me join the armed forces; she said I was too young (I was sixteen). Six months later I was drafted. I was trained as a code talker, but I didn't realize how important my job was at the time. My first experience was at Saipan, where every night, someone got killed."

Frank Chee Willetto and his father, Chee Willeto, eighty-nine.

FRANK CHEE WILLETTO

2nd Marine Division
SAIPAN
OKINAWA

"Before the war, I was a sheep herder. Then I enlisted on the advice of one of my teachers. The first time I fell into a foxhole with the enemy during the landing on Tarawa was a memorable occasion. Nearly getting our radio foxhole bombed at Guadalcanal also stands out in my memory."

WILLIAM DEAN WILSON
Ashiihi and Todikozi Clans

1st, 2nd, 5th Marine Divisions
GUADALCANAL
NEW ZEALAND
NEW HEBRIDES
TARAWA
HAWAII
SASEBO

VINCENT YAZZA
Naakaii Dine's and Tabaaha Clans
6th Marine Division

"I was drafted and trained in communications. I also acted as an interpreter."

LEMUEL B. YAZZIE
Tsi'naajinii and Kin yaa'aanii Clans

4th, 6th Marine Divisions
MAUI
GUAM
TSINTOS
CHINA

PAHE D. YAZZIE   *"I volunteered to serve my country."*
Todich'ii'nii and Tachii'nii Clans

5th Marine Division
NEW CALEDONIA
HAWAII
SAIPAN

"At one point on the front line in Iwo Jima, during a barrage of guns and rockets, we received orders by radio to assist in the rescue of our platoon, which was under fire. We did, and got all of our men safely back to our regiment."

RAPHAEL D. YAZZIE
Tachii'nii and Kinlichii'nii Clans

4th Marine Division
MARSHALL ISLANDS
SAIPAN
TINIAN
IWO JIMA

"We moved from place to place with our radios. Even if we were scared, we just went on until we finished our duty."

George Yoe and his grandson.

GEORGE EDWARD YOE
*Todich'ii'nii and
Honaghaahnii Clans*

4th Marine Division
SAIPAN
TINIAN
IWO JIMA
MAUI
CHINA

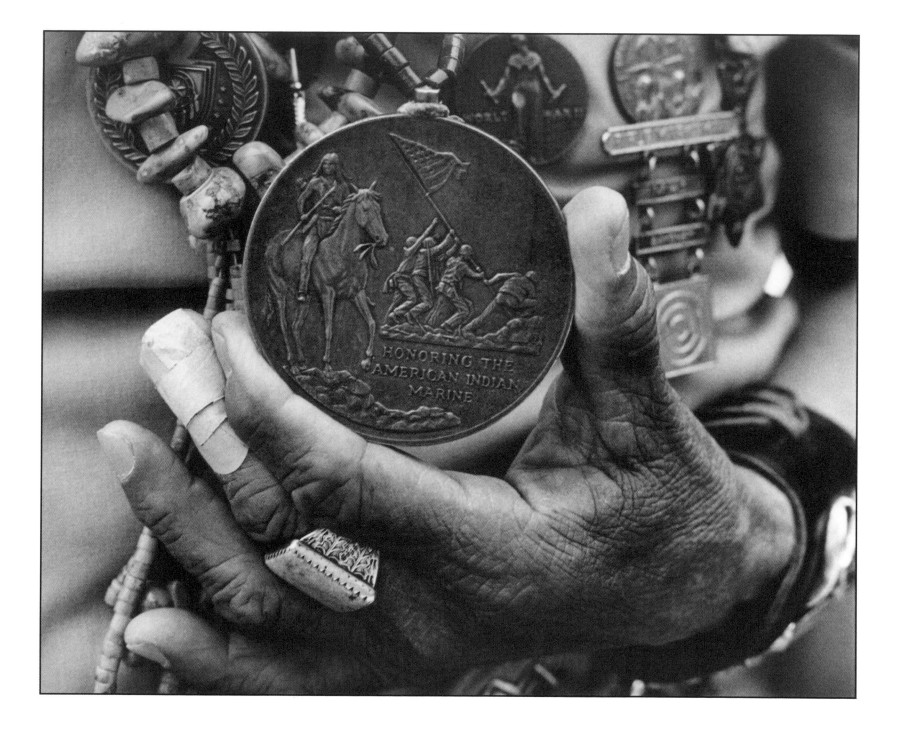

NAVAJO CLAN NAMES
with English Translation

Atsosi dine's	THE FEATHER PEOPLE
Ashiihi	THE SALT PEOPLE
Ashiihnii	THE SALT PEOPLE (EXTINCT)
Biih dine's	THE DEER PEOPLE
Biih bitoodnii	THE DEER SPRING PEOPLE
Biihtsoh dine's	THE BIG DEER PEOPLE
Bit'shnii	THE WITHIN-HIS-COVER PEOPLE
Bit'aa'nii	EXTINCT, NO ENGLISH TRANSLATION AVAILABLE
Deeshchii'nii	THE START-OF-THE-RED-STREAK PEOPLE
Dibe łizhini	THE BLACK SHEEP PEOPLE
Dichin dine's	THE HUNGER PEOPLE
Dzaaneez łani	THE MANY BURROS PEOPLE
Dsił na oodiłnii	THE TURNING MOUNTAIN PEOPLE

OPPOSITE: *Medal honoring the American Indian Marine; photograph taken in Phoenix, Arizona, 1989.*

Dziltl'ahni	THE MOUNTAIN RECESS PEOPLE
Dziltl'tade	THE NEAR MOUNTAIN PEOPLE
Dziltl'klanii	THE MOUNTAIN COVE PEOPLE
Gah dine's tachii'nii	THE RABBIT PEOPLE
Halt'sooi dine's	THE MEADOW PEOPLE
Hask'aa hadzoho	THE YUCCA FRUIT-STRUNG-OUT-IN-A-LINE PEOPLE
Hashtł'ishnii	THE MUD PEOPLE
Honaghaahnii	THE HE-WALKS-AROUND-ONE PEOPLE
Hooghan łani	THE MANY HOGANS PEOPLE
'Iich'ah dine's	THE PEOPLE THAT HAVE FITS
Jah'yaaloolii	THE STICKING-UP-EARS PEOPLE
K'aahanaanii	THE LIVING ARROW PEOPLE
K'ai'ch'ebaanii	THE LINE-OF-WILLOWS-EXTEND-OUT GRAY PEOPLE
Kin łichii'nii	THE RED HOUSE PEOPLE
Kin łitsonii	THE YELLOW HOUSE PEOPLE
Kin yaa'aanii	THE TOWERING HOUSE PEOPLE
Lok'aa'dine's	THE REED PEOPLE

104

Ma'ii deeshgiizhinii	THE COYOTE PASS PEOPLE; THE JEMEZ CLAN
Naaneesht'ezhi tachii ni	THE CHARCOAL-STREAKED DIVISION OF THE TACHII NI CLAN
Naakaii dine's	THE MEXICAN CLAN
Naashashi	THE BEAR ENEMIES; THE TEWA CLAN
Naashgali dine's	THE MESCALERO APACHE CLAN
Naasht'ezhi dine's	THE ZUNI CLAN
Naayizi dine's	THE SQUASH PEOPLE
Nat'ch dine's	THE TOBACCO PEOPLE
Nihcobaanii	THE GRAY-STREAK-ENDS PEOPLE
Nooda'i dine's	THE UTE CLAN
Nooda'i dine's tachii'nii	THE UTE DIVISION OF THE TACHII'NII CLAN
Sei bse hooghnaii	THE SAND HOGAN PEOPLE
Tabaaha	THE WATER'S EDGE PEOPLE
Tachii'nii	THE RED-RUNNING-INTO-THE-WATER PEOPLE
Ta'neezahnii	THE TANGLE PEOPLE
To dikozi	THE SALT WATER PEOPLE

To'ahani	THE NEAR-TO-WATER PEOPLE
To'aheedliinii	THE WATER-FLOWS-TOGETHER PEOPLE
To'azoli	THE LIGHT WATER PEOPLE
To'baazhni'azhi	THE TWO-CAME-TO-WATER PEOPLE
To dich'ii'nii	THE BITTER WATER PEOPLE
Totsohnii	THE BIG WATER PEOPLE
Tł'aashchi'i	THE RED BOTTOM PEOPLE
Tł'izi lani	THE MANY GOATS PEOPLE
Tł'ogi	THE HAIRY ONES (?); THE WEAVERS (?); THE ZIA
Ts'ah yisk'idnii	THE SAGE BRUSH HILL PEOPLE
Tse deeshgizhnii	THE ROCK GAP PEOPLE
Tse nahabiłnii or *Tse nahadilnii*	*MEANING UNKNOWN*
Tse njikini	THE HONEY-COMBED ROCK PEOPLE
Tse taa'aanii	THE ROCK-EXTENDS-INTO-WATER PEOPLE
Tsezhin ndii'aai	THE SLANTED-LAVA-SPIRE PEOPLE
Tseikeehe	THE TWO-ROCKS-SIT PEOPLE

Tsi'naajinii	*MEANING UNKNOWN*
Tsin sikaadnii	THE CLUMPED TREE PEOPLE
Tsin yideełcoi	THE TREE STRETCHER PEOPLE
Ye'ii dine's	THE MONSTER PEOPLE
Yoo'o dine's	THE BEAD PEOPLE

Kenji Kawano is a native-born Japanese who came to America in 1973 and was drawn to the mystery and beauty of the Navajo Reservation, where he met Carl Gorman, one of the patriarchs of the Navajo Code Talkers Association. His interest and their trust led to his appointment as the group's official photographer, and his portraits are honest and sensitive representations.

Benis M. Frank is head of the Marine Corps Oral History Program, Marine Corps History and Museums Divisions, USMC Headquarters. He served as an enlisted Marine in World War II, participating in the invasions of Peleliu and Okinawa and the occupation of North China with the 1st Marine Division. He also served with that division later in Korea, where he was the Division Order of Battle Officer, and Battalion Intelligence Officer of the 2nd Battalion, 5th Marines. Mr. Frank is the author of numerous books, including *Okinawa, Touchstone to Victory, Okinawa: The Great Island Battle,* and *Halsey,* among others. He and his wife live in Bowie, Maryland.